"I" CAN RELATE

How Not to Lose Yourself in Relationships

Kenyatta,

Thank you for your support, and May God bless you with much love in all your relationships.

Wanda

Wanda L. Scott

Nicole L. Wade, Editor
Cover Design by Lazarus Graphics
Photos by **Ms. DIG** Nora Canfield
Inside Layout and Design by Wanda L. Scott

Paperback ISBN-13: 978-0-9761322-4-0
eBook ISBN-13: 978-0-9761322-7-1

10 9 8 7 6 5 4 3 2 1

Printed in the Unites States of America

Table of Contents

As you read this book it is my hope that you will have those moments when you say out loud *"I" can relate!* I know there will also be those moments when you will silently shake your head and say inside, *"I" wish I couldn't relate.* See relationships are challenging for us all, especially if we are trying to please God and love one another. Relationships are also great and we long for them, God created us that way. So as you read and declare "I" can relate, just know that there is hope in the Lord, and **that** revelation is a start toward better relationships.

Keep a journal of your *"I can relate"* moments as you read!

INTRODUCTION
The God Influence

GOD IS A GOD OF RELATIONSHIP. In your God experience, the first relationship that is supposed to develop is the one between you and God. We are supposed to love God with all our heart, all our mind, all our soul and strength. This takes a lot of time, effort, and sacrifice. As we learn to do this we learn about relationship. Relationship is what this book is all about. Specifically, we will discuss your "**I**" and its place in relationships.

As we move through the chapters of this book, we will literally take a journey through the letters in:
R E L A T I O N S H I P
Using the wisdom in the word of God, we will take the "**I**", and work around it with the other letters in order to see how the Lord can guide us in relationship. The only letter in RELATIONSHIP that does not have its own chapter is the letter **L**. We address the L here, because it stands for *Love*. God is love. God proclaims in His word that He is love. There is no good relationship if it does not have love. Therefore, there is no good relationship without God in it, and His love to guide it. So we must go into every relationship putting God first by letting Him, by His Holy Spirit lead us and guide us in, through and sometimes out of relationship with people, places and things. This book will concentrate on *relationship in respect to people*.

In life the first relationship we ever have is with our *self*. Unknowingly we can either base this relationship, or our understanding of "**I**" on how others treat us, or on how others say we should be treated. Depending on the influences in our lives, this understanding could cause positive or negative actions, emotions or behaviors associated with how we treat our *self*.

How do you treat your "I"?

That question is eternally impacted by whether or not we get to know the Creator God. Just like we consult the owner's manual on a product we buy, we need to consult God because He created us uniquely, and to be in relationship. In knowing our creator/owner, we learn about our *self*, and the truth about how we should treat ourselves. God is the most positive influence of truth that we can have, and any actions, emotions, or behaviors we learn from Him will instruct us in the best relationship possible. As we know God and grow in relationship with Him, we get to know our **"I"**, and how "fearfully and wonderfully" we are made. This God influence is the only Truth that starts with growth in our relationship with God. It then grows in *Love* so that we can know our *self*, and then overflows into every other relationship we have in our *life*.

"The most important aspect of Christianity is not the work we do, but the relationship we maintain and the surrounding influence and qualities produced by that relationship. That is all God asks us to give our attention to, and it is the one thing that is continually under attack." — Oswald Chambers, My Utmost for His Highest

Who has influenced you?
God wants to…

What has defined you?
Until you read God's word,
You won't know the truth.

What do you think of yourself?
You were created by God himself.

His love will define you.

His love should influence you.

His love is always thinking of you.

His love is waiting on you.

WLS

1

The "I"
RELAT"I"ONSHIP

A S WE DECLARED IN THE INTRODUCTION, God is a God of relationship. He desires for us to put our "I" in relationship with Him first, so He can add other relationships into our lives. As we grow in the grace and knowledge of our Lord, He can do a perfecting work in ALL our relationships – present and future. God is the God of our yesterdays, today, and tomorrows. *Knowing and growing in Him is the key to knowing our "I".*

Our entire life is made up of relationships. The most important relationship should be with God, and the rest of the relationships that we form will fall in line with the maturity or depth of our relationship with God. Our vertical relationship with God defines our horizontal relationships with Man. In other words, how much we know about God, love God, and follow Jesus, shows in how we deal with other people. Each relationship we have should be developed in love. We only know this love if we have been shown this love by God and the sacrifice of His Son Jesus Christ.

Getting to know the Lord in relationship, directly corresponds with the moral code laid out in the Ten Commandments that offers us guidance on how our actions should 'be' or 'not be' in relationship with God and others. Believing in and accepting a relationship with Jesus Christ is the only way to truly fulfill or adhere to the tenants of the commandments.

Matthew 5:[17] [Christ Fulfills the Law] "Do not think that I came to destroy the Law or the Prophets. I did not come to destroy but to fulfill. (NKJV)

Romans 8:[3] The Law of Moses cannot do this, because our selfish desires make the Law weak. But God set you free when he sent his own Son to be like us sinners and to be a sacrifice for our sin. God used Christ's body to condemn sin. [4] He did this, so that we would do what the Law commands by obeying the Spirit instead of our own desires. [5] People who are ruled by their desires think only of themselves. Everyone who is ruled by the Holy Spirit thinks about spiritual things. (CEV)

The first five commandments deal with our relationship with God, and the second five deal with our relationship with others. When the first five manifest *consistently* in our life toward God, then there will be a propensity toward the other five manifesting in our life toward others. When we understand the God of Love, put Him first, revere & respect Him as the Lord of our life, knowing the vast love He has demonstrated for and toward us,

Our entire life is made up of relationships.

only then can we love like He loves us. When we love ourselves like He loves us, then that love can be translated through the Holy Spirit as love toward one another. The power to adhere to these commandments will only manifest through relationship with Jesus Christ.

Romans 13:[8] Owe nothing to anyone—except for your obligation to love one another. If you love your neighbor, you will fulfill the requirements of God's law. [9] For the commandments say, "You must not commit adultery. You must not murder. You must not steal. You must not covet." These—and other such commandments—are summed up in this one commandment: "Love your neighbor as yourself."[10] Love does no wrong to others, so love fulfills the requirements of God's law. (NLT)

Without the power of the Lord's Holy Spirit we cannot keep the Law. Jesus left us the Holy Spirit when He ascended to heaven, so that we might have God's power living inside of us. (John 14:26 AMP) In the Law sin abounds, but grace and truth came through Jesus Christ and empowers us over sin through faith to holiness.

John 14:[26] But the Comforter (Counselor, Helper, Intercessor, Advocate, Strengthener, Standby), the Holy Spirit, Whom the Father will send in My name [in My place, to represent Me and act on My behalf], He will teach you all things. And He will cause you to recall (will remind you of, bring to your remembrance) everything I have told you. (AMP)

God
Jesus

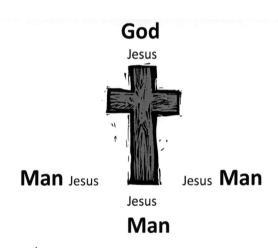

Man Jesus   Jesus **Man**

Jesus
Man

Romans 7:[4] So, my dear brothers and sisters, this is the point: You died to the power of the law when you died with Christ. And now you are united with the one who was raised from the dead. As a result, we can produce a harvest of good deeds for God. [5] When we were controlled by our old nature, sinful desires were at work within us, and the law aroused these evil desires that produced a harvest of sinful deeds, resulting in death. [6] But now we have been released from the law, for we died to it and are no longer captive to its power. Now we can serve God, not in the old way of obeying the letter of the law, but in the new way of living in the Spirit. (NLT)

Motives -vs- Intentions of the Heart

Our faith in Jesus should drive us to want to know this self-sacrificing God. This knowing in relationship will bring us to holiness in Him, not by anything we wear, say or do. It is an unconscious working of God in us through the power of His word. As the word of God working in us transforms our "I", we grow in our understanding of our *self* in respect to God, and then we learn how to manage the "flesh" when it tries to place itself over the will of God for our lives. The ability to manage comes as our relationship grows with the Lord Jesus Christ. The word "Lord" can mean ruler, master, or head. If Jesus is our Lord, then God's way of doing things must become our way of doing things. God's thoughts about us must be our thoughts about us. God's love for people must be shown in our love for people. God's hatred of sin must be our hatred of sin. Only in our understanding of how our flesh, this earthly suit, fights against the Spirit of God in us, will we know how much we need God to help us in our relationship with our *self*.

> **God's thoughts about us must be our thoughts about us.**

Galatians 5:[16] So I say, let the Holy Spirit guide your lives. Then you won't be doing what your sinful nature craves. [17] The sinful nature wants to do evil, which is just the opposite of what the Spirit wants. And the Spirit gives us desires that are the opposite of what the sinful nature desires. These two forces are constantly fighting each other, so you are not free to carry out your good intentions. [18] But when you are directed by the Spirit, you are not under obligation to the law of Moses. (NLT)

In verse 17 of Galatians 5, it says that because of the desires of our sinful nature we "are not free to carry out our good intentions". The next verse starts with a "but"....I love it when God's word gives us an alternative to be free. When we are led, guided, and directed by the Holy Spirit, we are free to "carry out our good intentions" because they are

God's intentions. Then we are empowered by God, and strengthened by the Holy Spirit's guidance. This is such good news! We can sometimes walk around from day to day like there is no power to do what is right in God's eyes. We often feel that "**I**" just can't do this, but with God all things are possible if we choose to obey Him!

If you look at the definition of the word *intention* as defined on dictionary.com, it says that it is:

- an act or instance of determining mentally upon some action or result.
- the end or object intended; purpose.

So if we intend to or have an intention to do something, we have mentally purposed to perform or do that action to a certain end or objective. We must have thought about it and determined that the end would be beneficial, if it was a good intention. God always has "good" in mind for us. He works all things together for our good. Every good and perfect gift comes from Him. He wants us to have good success. The difference in what God would define as a good intention and what we call good, can hinge on a little word called motive.

Motive is defined on dictionary.com as:

- something that causes a person to act in a certain way, do a certain thing,
- the goal or object of a person's actions

God's motives are always pure, good and of love. They have been proven and are sure. Our motives as humans are not so. Different things cause us to act a certain way. We are motivated by such things as emotions, physical pain, or other people. Our motives can be good or bad, and sometimes it is hard to distinguish what our true intention or motive is. We can be blinded by our motivations, due to many things that we have been exposed to in this world. Life has a way of hurting us and clouding our hearts to the love that we are supposed to show because others have not shown that love to us. The good news is that as we have been discussing the

Spirit of God, which always has good intentions and pure motives, and can help us clear the cloudiness and mend our broken hearts. With God, our intentions can be based on a pure motive, if we mentally determine to set them before God before we act on them. Knowing the struggle between the flesh and the spirit, it is wise to seek God's guidance so that the spirit will win. God is called the mender of broken hearts (Psalm 147:3), and His love will ease the pain of this life and give us overcoming power. God's word calls for us to guard our hearts, because out of it flows the issues of life. This process of checking our motivation with the Lord's help, keeps us out of unintentional situations that make up the life issues that we need to guard our heart from. This process also helps us to perfect our relationship with the Lord, so that we consistently realize our need for Him in every action. In this we continue to learn how to love ourselves by eliminating the pain in our life, and seeking God for His ever-loving guidance. We then can turn this into an act of love toward one another. This God empowered love fulfills the law and will help us discern our intent versus the motivations of our hearts.

We are motivated by such things as emotions, physical pain, or other people.

"Right" Relationship with the Lord

We could write chapters on what it means to be "right" with God. Humans have doctrinal books written by denominations that express their personal scriptural definitions of "how" to be right with God. Christians can also have opinions about being "right" before God, but there is only one understanding that matters….God's.

God sent Jesus to die on the cross, and be raised again with ALL power in His hand, in order for humans to have a chance at being in "right" relationship with Him again since the fall of Adam and Eve (Genesis 3). The word of God gives clear definition of what God expects of those who confess and believe in Jesus Christ throughout scripture. This starts from the obedience of Abraham, to the giving of the commandments, to the fulfillment of them in Jesus Christ. From there we see the call for repentance and the act of following Jesus. Then the word of God also calls for us to grow in the grace and knowledge of God, rejoicing and praying always. It is also clear in the word of God that obedience and humility bring God near. His grace provides the power and His blessings help us to overcome.

The word of God uses a term called "imputed" righteousness (Romans 4:10-12). This just means that God has granted us or placed in us, His righteousness through Jesus Christ when we accept Him as our Lord and Savior and repent of our sins. Through Jesus, God sees us as being "right" with Him. We have the right to have a relationship with Him. We are in "right" relationship with Him through the blood shed by Jesus on the cross. We have a blood bought covenant with God that says we are His and He is ours. We are loved, and have a right to call to Him, call on Him and have His presence in our lives through worship, bible study and prayer. We have the right to have a God who is not far off, but near to us in our hearts. With this right, we have the gift of the in-dwelling Holy Spirit that guides us so that we can know our *self* through a God who loves us.

Romans 8:[1]So now there is no condemnation for those who belong to Christ Jesus. [2] And because you belong to him, the power of the life-giving Spirit has freed you from the power of sin that leads to death. [3] The law of Moses was unable to save us because of the weakness of our sinful nature. So God did what the law could not do. He sent his own Son in a body like the bodies we sinners have. And in that body God declared an end to sin's control over us by giving his Son as a sacrifice for our sins. [4] He did this so that the just requirement of the law would be fully satisfied for us, who no longer follow our sinful nature but instead follow the Spirit. [5] Those who are dominated by the sinful nature think about sinful things, but those who are controlled by the Holy Spirit think about things that please the Spirit. (NLT)

"I" Can Relate

"We are only what we are in the dark; all the rest is reputation. What God looks at is what we are in the dark—the imaginations of our minds; the thoughts of our heart; the habits of our bodies; these are the things that mark us in God's sight." *The Love of God —* Oswald Chambers in *The Ministry of the Unnoticed*

This is one of those areas that "I" can really relate to more than I care to admit. I think the older I get the more I try not to question myself and why I do things. "I" am grown right! Nope. I am always God's child and I have to be chastened, slowed down, and even stopped sometimes because I am going full speed ahead not checking my motivation in the situation. And to make things worse, I can initially clean up my intentions to make them seem pure, but then the Holy Spirit will start pressing in on me and I will feel uneasy......got me again. As much as I cringe when I get that feeling, I am thankful that I serve a God who loves me and cares about me that much to participate that intimately in my life. The Lord wants to be involved with me to help me decipher between what I should do and what I want to do, and what my true intentions are in that moment. Whew, my "I" is a trip sometimes. I am so thankful God still loves me and gently or not so gently guides me back on track. Even when "I" don't stop. Even when I am convicted, the Lord will still forgive me when I ask and He will help me work my way out of the situation when I repent. There is even grace when I have to suffer the consequences! God is so amazing. He knows...

15

Who am I?

What role do I play?

Am I important....
In the relationships I participate in day to day?

What can I give?
I can give my heart to Christ,
....a gift that is without price.

How should I live?
With God's love I can relate,
with God's love I can change my fate.

WLS

2

REL "AT"IONSHIP

Ask Yourself 'Where Am I "AT" right now?

THIS IS ONE OF THE HARDEST QUESTIONS to decipher truthfully about ourselves. Our emotions can play tricks on us depending on what is going on in our lives. If we are not physically healthy, whether that means feeding and taking care of our bodies, or that we have sicknesses, this can skew our understanding of what we are capable of. Spiritually we might think we are in tune with the Lord, but we might have become comfortable in our religious routine. With all this said, it might sound impossible to know where we are "AT", but we must always remember that with God all things are possible.

Therein lies the beauty of having a "right" relationship with God. It it seems that we should be able to decipher where we are "AT" emotionally, spiritually and physically, but can we? Whether it is our emotions, physical disability, or spiritual deficiency, they can feed into our sinful nature and be in opposition to God's spirit. God speaks of this opposition in the book of Galatians.

Galatians 5:[16] So I say, let the Holy Spirit guide your lives. Then you won't be doing what your sinful nature craves. [17] The sinful nature wants to do evil, which is just the opposite of what the Spirit wants. And the Spirit gives us desires that are the opposite of what the sinful nature desires. These two forces are constantly fighting each other, so you are not free to carry out your good intentions. (NLT)

Paul being inspired by the Holy Spirit talks about the flesh being contrary to the spirit. This simply means that there is a fight going on as long as we are in this flesh, or earthly suit. The flesh wants to win, but the Spirit has the power to overcome IF we choose to obey. As the word of God also says, who can know the mind of a man, but the spirit of that man?

1 Corinthians 2:[11] No one can know a person's thoughts except that person's own spirit, and no one can know God's thoughts except God's own Spirit. (NLT)

In the same respect, who can know the mind of God, but the Spirit of God? So we must *walk in* or *act according to* what God says by His Holy Spirit, and not be at the whim of what our flesh feels at the moment; whether that is an emotional or physical reaction. If our flesh is fighting against our spirit, which should be in-line with the Spirit of God, we can be confused. We need to be in communion with the Lord through prayer, bible study and fellowship with other believers in order to stay aware of our current situation. So let's explore how to seek the Lord in each of these areas, in order to know where we are "**AT**" in each one.

> We must not be at the whim of what our flesh feels at the moment; whether that is an emotional or physical reaction.

Emotionally (*Feelings*)

Proverbs 29:[11] A fool vents all his feelings, but a wise man holds them back. (NKJV)

Have you heard the saying that our faith has nothing to do with our feelings? Well, that statement has basis in the fact that we cannot let our emotions or feelings, change our actions in accordance with our faith. Emotions and/or feelings are part of our soul. The soul is made up of our mind, will and heart (emotions). These emotions or feelings are rooted in prior experiences, good or bad. These emotions can typically drive us to react according to that past experience instead of the current situation. These emotions can also trigger a desire to grab on to something that is comfortable or familiar. This can be very dangerous as a child of God. We are called to live in the newness of God, thinking according to a renewed mind in the word of God and with actions in accordance with the fruit of the Spirit. In order to keep our emotions in check, we have to identify our triggers. Triggers are unique to each of us based on our dealings in this world.

Emotional Triggers
One of the most important things for us to do for our *self* is to ask God to help us identify our emotional triggers. By triggers, I mean the things that cause us to act out of character. The things that make us go against our new life (the new man) in Christ. These triggers make us choose to act or walk in the flesh, instead of operating in the Spirit by the power of God. If these triggers are identified, then we can have a better understanding of where we are "**AT**", so we will know how to govern ourselves in all of our current or potential relationships.

Emotional triggers can be, but are not limited to "feeling like we are out of control in some area of our *life*", "feeling frustrated, tired, or weary", "feeling overwhelmed", "feeling like life has passed us by", etc. These triggers are usually set by the world's timelines, by cultural or familial mindsets that we have learned, and finally by allowing others expectations to weigh on our minds. We will sometimes tell ourselves that we should have had a certain job by this age, and if we don't we might consider ourselves a failure by the worlds standards. The key is to remember that as a child of God He has written our whole life before we were even born, and has a plan and purpose for our life that might not look like the worlds timetable. Or you might think that you are too old to have the child you thought would be in your future. So you marry the first man you see and have a baby, or you decide to "find a sperm donor" and sin by fornicating to fulfill your own agenda according to a cultural or worldly expectation. Like Sarah (Genesis) and Elizabeth (Luke), what God wills is outside of man's time, and with Him all things are possible. Or maybe you are the problem, and because of past circumstances in your life you are a "control freak", and things just don't seem to be going according to your plan in any area of your life. As a child of God, the Lord has been known to design

These triggers are usually set by the world's timeline, cultural or familial mindsets and by allowing others expectations to weigh on our minds.

certain situations and allow certain things to happen to us called trials that are meant to bring us to a better realization and understanding of God's power and sovereignty in our lives. God loves us and wants us to KNOW Him in truth, superseding every trigger and wrong expectation we have functioning in our lives. When we ask God to show us these emotional triggers and wrong expectations, He will faithfully and lovingly show us with divine orchestration an answer that is fit just for us bringing our "I" to a place of peace in Him. Only then will we overcome our emotions to see clearly where we are "AT", helping us to know if it is God's best for us to engage in relationship.

Each emotional trigger has to be dealt with at the root. Only God can show us the real reason why we are triggered to act out of our flesh when we emotionally feel that way. Men and women both have these emotional triggers, resulting from unique experiences in their lives, and causing unique responses. No human is exempt. The good news is that as a child of God, we are not alone. As a child of God Jesus will empower us to find the truth and set us free from fleshly responses. Jesus died and was raised again so that we would have overcoming power from the wounds of the world, and the grace for Him to mend our hearts so that we can live according to the fruit of His Spirit. When we accept God's help we place ourselves in a position close to Him, which means that we can treat others we are in relationship with according to His love.

Take, for example when a woman is on her menstrual cycle, medicine has shown proof of the hormonal imbalances that can happen in her body. This time in a women's life is a perfect example of when emotions can cause triggers that impact her relationships. God created women and designed her to have a menstrual cycle for the great privilege of birthing children. If He designed her, He knows the impact of this emotional time in her life. So God can also empower her to stay in character that is pleasing to Him during these times. God can help women to manage their flesh to remain loving in relationship.

Ask God to help you identify your emotional triggers.

Men are not exempt from heightened emotional times. Their emotions are most often triggered by physical impairments that can prompt emotional triggers. Men still have emotional responses outside of the physical. We are all human and subject to the flesh, but God intentionally designed us differently to come together in harmony in these unique differences. The male/female relationship is divine and fulfills God's design for family, creating children in His image and likeness.

21

Physically

When we as men and women are physically impaired in some way, whether we are injured physically or physically impaired through mal-nutrition or disease, the physical impairment can cloud our judgment. Take for instance a man who has labored most of his life with his hands or in his physical strength. Loss of that ability can have a drastic impact on his capacity to be in relationship. If this man cannot work, whether that be in areas such as construction, boxing, landscaping or driving a truck, he could possibly feel useless, incompetent, or unproductive. This physical loss can then cause an emotional trigger. The man needs the Lord to guide him toward the "new" way of doing life. He needs to understand whether he can do what he used to do or not, God still has a plan and a purpose for this time or season in his life. God's grace and peace can help him transition into a more stable place internally, in order to be able to function with love in a relationship.

> Whether injured physically or physically-impaired through malnutrition or disease, each can cloud our judgment.

Another example is of our soldiers who sacrifice their physical lives for our freedom, and then can come home without some part of their physical abilities. Hopefully they already have a relationship with the Lord, but if not He is always waiting. They have to seek God for guidance in this process to redefine what life will look like for them after war. Both of these situations can directly impact our pride. Physical impairment can lead to loss of a job, loss of pay, and loss of self-esteem. When this physical impairment causes a loss, the source of our livelihood can be taken away. Any of these alone or together can be a recipe for dysfunction in relationships. When what has given us pride in the past is taken away, we can be disoriented in who or what our purpose is. What we believed to be our source has distracted us from our true source. This false source in which we found pride, can also be taken away to humble us and point us back to what our real source and dependence should be.....God. Humility is needed. That humility can bring us to our knees, in the best position to get

Any of these alone or together can be a recipe for dysfunction.

the re-direction for the new life we can have regardless of the physical impairment. When we are in this humble position before God, our relationship with Him grows and our "I" grows in understanding. Only then are we back in position to be in relationship with others. If you are operating in relationship with God, His Spirit will guide you to those who can understand and handle you where you are.

Spiritually

One of the worst times to pursue a new or old relationship is when you are spiritually "low". By *low* I mean you feel like you have not been pleasing to the Lord in your choices (*condemnation*), and have not sincerely repented (*which is different from asking for forgiveness*). Or you feel

Discontentment is dangerous.

frustrated spiritually about your progress or the place you are in your life; discontentment is dangerous and takes our trust off of God and puts it in our own understanding. And lastly, when you have not been in the word of God, studying, listening to teaching, or praying before the Lord your spirit can be starved or deprived of the food it needs (*God's word*). These are just some examples of situations when we might not be hearing from God clearly, thus not being able to pull from His strength to make the right choices. If we are not hearing clearly from God, we don't know where we are

"**AT**". Remember our current relationship with God is the barometer for how well we will or can deal with others.

I like this example in 1 Samuel chapter 12 when the children of Israel have asked for a king like the other nations around them. This offended God, because the children of Israel were a chosen and special people to God, He was their King. When the children of Israel realize what they have done, they are fearful, and this is God's response to them through the prophet Samuel:

1 Samuel 12: [20] And Samuel said to the people, Fear not. You have indeed done all this evil; yet turn not aside from following the Lord, but serve Him with all your heart. [21] And turn not aside after vain and worthless things which cannot profit or deliver you, for they are empty and futile. [22] The Lord will not forsake His people for His great name's sake, for it has pleased Him to make you a people for Himself. (AMP)

In this example, the people know they have done wrong, or made a wrong choice. God encourages them to not turn away from Him, but still serve Him whole heartedly. See God knows how we are in this flesh. We don't understand His love and faithfulness to us, even when we are not faithful. If we just ask for forgiveness, and turn

When weary in spirit, don't take your eyes off of God's mercy and grace.

from the evil we have done (repent), God is right there ready to be near us, with us and continue to guide us back to where we need to be. When we are weary in spirit, we can lose heart and take our eyes off of the wonderful mercy and grace of God. We must re-focus and believe that God will never leave us or forsake us, even in our wrong doing. The good work He starts in us, He will complete until the day Jesus returns (1 Phil. 1:6). Only then will we spiritually see clearly where we are "**AT**", and if we or the person we are in relationship with is fit for us at that moment.

Understanding where we are spiritually can be very tricky. If we judge our relationship with God solely based on our own opinion, we are acting in isolation, and God never called for us to be alone in this life as a child of God. We are born again spiritually into a family with other children of God.

We need other children of God to challenge our thinking, bring conviction, and open our hearts for change, growth & maturity. We are born spiritually as a member of the body of Christ, so that we must function together in unity to accomplish God's purposes. When we don't have other trusted, spiritually mature followers of Christ to help encourage us, rightly divide the word with us, and pray for and with us, we can be misguided by our own perceptions, worldly influences, and fleshly opinions. Man looks at the outside, but God knows the intentions of the heart. If we judge others, by those same standards we will be judged. We need children of God outside of us to challenge our thinking, bring conviction, and open our hearts for the Lord to show us our need to change, grow and mature. God has people and places for our lives. He has divine connections, encounters and relationships to pull and push us spiritually toward truth, shielded by His grace. We have to be open spiritually to the word of God so that we will understand where we are "**AT**", and be guided to where God wants us. Only then will our relationships be fruitful the way the Lord desires for us.

Active Relationships
Is it smart/safe to be in relationship where I am "AT" right now?

Now that we have looked to the word of God for guidance in understanding where we are "AT" in these three areas, we can make better decisions about whether we need to be in different kinds of relationships. We always have to be in "right" relationship with the Lord, nurturing and valuing our time with Him. This is the foundation for every other relationship. There are also other relationships that we have to manage, that might seem like they are impossible to avoid. Some of these

> This choice to engage in relationship has the potential to give us more heart issues, hurt others, and infect our life with sin.

involuntary relationships could be with our mothers, fathers, siblings, spouses, children or co-workers. A lot of the time it can be almost impossible to not come in contact with these types of relationships. These involuntary relationships can be beautiful and loving. But there might be times when one of them is not. Even though you might have to be in contact with them (*involuntary*), you can still be smart and guard your heart through the wisdom of Christ Jesus.

Matthew 12 [47] Someone told Jesus, "Your mother and your brothers are standing outside, and they want to speak to you." [48] Jesus asked, "Who is my mother? Who are my brothers?" [49] Then he pointed to his disciples and said, "Look, these are my mother and brothers. [50] Anyone who does the will of my Father in heaven is my brother and sister and mother!" (NLT)

We have to keep the Lord's words in perspective so that we can regard those who are our blood by birth family, those who we are *involuntarily* in relationship with in the light of our new birth by the Spirit into the family of God.

Titus 3 [4] But—When God our Savior revealed his kindness and love, [5] he saved us, not because of the righteous things we had done, but because of his mercy. He washed away our sins, giving us a new birth and new life through the Holy Spirit. [6] He generously poured out the Spirit upon us through Jesus Christ our Savior. (NLT)

We are to love regardless. We know that "For God so loved the world that He gave his only begotten Son." So we are to show love to everyone as a child of God, but not to the point of compromising who we are in Christ and the knowledge that we are fearfully and wonderfully made. Even in our involuntary relationships we have the ability to limit our exposure to that person. We also have wisdom from God on how and when to interact with them. The Lord can give us the power to temper our responses and still show love as an example of His presence in our lives. We are not obligated to be abused or misused by any involuntary relationship. God can provide us a way of escape, and He can and does have power over those who don't follow Him. God is sovereign and can control all creation as He sees fit. We need to be confident enough in our relationship with the Lord to trust Him and allow Him to deal with us and any of our involuntary relationships the way He deems necessary.

Use the freedom in Christ to make wise decisions.

Also there are other *voluntary* relationships that we open ourselves up to or obligate ourselves to such as friendships and dating relationships. Please notice that I used the words, *"open ourselves up to"* and *"obligate ourselves to"*. These can be dangerous situations, but they are individual choices that we make when we do not use the freedom we have in Christ to make wise decisions. This is not a safe place to be in if we have not carefully evaluated where we are "**AT**" *in light of our emotions, our physical state or spiritual mindset.* This choice to engage in relationship has the potential to give us more heart issues, hurt others, and open the door for the enemy to infect our *life* with sin. Let's look at some biblical examples of obligating and opening ourselves up to relationships that were not in God's will for our lives, and could have been avoided with a proper perspective of where our "**I**" is "**AT**".

Lust (Male/Female)

King David is a good example of persons who opened themselves up to a relationship and made an unwise choice in his dealings with Bathsheba. David hurt others and his life was infected with sin.

2 Samuel 11 [1] In the spring of the year, when kings normally go out to war, David sent Joab and the Israelite army to fight the Ammonites. They destroyed the Ammonite army and laid siege to the city of Rabbah. However, David stayed behind in Jerusalem. [2] Late one afternoon, after his midday rest, David got out of bed and was walking on the roof of the palace. As he looked out over the city, he noticed a woman of unusual beauty taking a bath. [3] He sent someone to find out who she was, and he was told, "She is Bathsheba, the daughter of Eliam and the wife of Uriah the Hittite." [4] Then David sent messengers to get her; and when she came to the palace, he slept with her. She had just completed the purification rites after having her menstrual period. Then she returned home. [5] Later, when Bathsheba discovered that she was pregnant, she sent David a message, saying, "I'm pregnant." (NLT)

The bible does not fully tell us what David's mindset was or where he was "**AT**" mentally, but we do know that he was supposed to be out at war with his army. David's behavior also leads us to believe that he might not have been spiritually "**AT**" the right place to engage in relationship. David was idle or had time on his hands that he normally would not. We as children of God can also find ourselves starting voluntary relationships when we are bored or idle, not busy doing what we are supposed to do. David walked into a lustful relationship which was clearly not in God's will for his life.

2 Samuel 12[1]So the LORD sent Nathan the prophet to tell David this story: "There were two men in a certain town. One was rich, and one was poor. [2] The rich man owned a great many sheep and cattle. [3] The poor man owned nothing but one little lamb he had bought. He raised that little lamb, and it grew up with his children. It ate from the man's own plate and drank from his cup. He cuddled it in his arms like a baby daughter. [4] One day a guest arrived at the home of the rich man. But instead of killing an animal from his own flock or herd, he took the poor man's lamb and killed it and prepared it for his guest."[5] David was furious. "As surely as the LORD lives," he vowed, "any man who would do such a thing deserves to die! [6] He must repay four lambs to the poor man for the one he stole and for having no pity." [7] Then Nathan said to David, "You are that man! The LORD, the God of Israel, says: I anointed you king of Israel and saved you from the power of Saul. [8] I gave you your master's house and his wives and the kingdoms of Israel and Judah. And if that had not been enough, I would have given you much, much more. [9] Why, then, have you despised the word of the LORD and done this horrible deed? For you have murdered Uriah the Hittite with the sword of the Ammonites and stolen his wife. [10] From this time on, your family will live by the sword because you have despised me by taking Uriah's wife to be your own.

Wrong Counsel (Friendships)

Amnon and Jonadab are examples of a voluntary relationship that shows when a man is emotionally and spiritually not "AT" the right place he can seek wrong counsel in friendships. Amnon chose to trust Jonadab when he was only his cousin, and was not obligated to listen to him.

2 Samuel 13 [1] Now David's son Absalom had a beautiful sister named Tamar. And Amnon, her half brother, fell desperately in love with her. [2] Amnon became so obsessed with Tamar that he became ill. She was a virgin, and Amnon thought he could never have her. [3] But Amnon had a very crafty friend—his cousin Jonadab. He was the son of David's brother Shimea. [4] One day

Jonadab said to Amnon, "What's the trouble? Why should the son of a king look so dejected morning after morning?" So Amnon told him, "I am in love with Tamar, my brother Absalom's sister." [5] "Well," Jonadab said, "I'll tell you what to do.............

God gives us the power to choose our friends with His guidance. God's word says in **Proverbs 18:**[24] A man who has friends must himself be friendly, But there is a friend who sticks closer than a brother. (NKJV)

[24] There are "friends" who destroy each other, but a real friend sticks closer than a brother. (NLT)

[24] Friends come and friends go, but a true friend sticks by you like family. The Message

I used all three versions of the same scripture, because each breaks down how friendship *can be*. What stands out to me in all three is how we have to be a friend first, and then also how the friendship is brought to a familial sense....a brother (or sister). Now look at these verses:

Proverbs 12:[26] The righteous should choose his friends carefully, For the way of the wicked leads them astray. (NKJV)

[26] The godly give good advice to their friends; the wicked lead them astray. (NLT)

[26] A good person survives misfortune, but a wicked life invites disaster. The Message

The word says that we have to *choose friends carefully*. Verse 26 also shows us that if we choose wrong, or a wicked person, we will be led astray and have disaster invited into our lives. The word of God brings such clarity for every aspect of our lives. God loves us so much that He will give us wisdom to choose the right friends. These friends should be our brothers and sisters in Christ, in the family of God. Even within the family of God, the body of Christ, we have to use wisdom and be guided by the Holy Spirit. Friends give grace, encourage one another, and provide good advice from the word of God. By the love and friendship of God, we can be a good friend and choose our friends wisely. If we don't, the continuation of this story will show how devastating it can be if we don't consult God in His word and call the wrong people friend opening ourselves up to wrong counsel.

5 "Well," Jonadab said, "I'll tell you what to do. Go back to bed and pretend you are ill. When your father comes to see you, ask him to let Tamar come and prepare some food for you. Tell him you'll feel better if she prepares it as you watch and feeds you with her own hands." 6 So Amnon lay down and pretended to be sick. And when the king came to see him, Amnon asked him, "Please let my sister Tamar come and cook my favorite dish as I watch. Then I can eat it from her own hands." 7 So David agreed and sent Tamar to Amnon's house to prepare some food for him. 8 When Tamar arrived at Amnon's house, she went to the place where he was lying down so he could watch her mix some dough. Then she baked his favorite dish for him. 9 But when she set the serving tray before him, he refused to eat.

There are other *voluntary* relationships that we *open ourselves up to* or *obligate ourselves to*.

"Everyone get out of here," Amnon told his servants. So they all left.

10 Then he said to Tamar, "Now bring the food into my bedroom and feed it to me here." So Tamar took his favorite dish to him. 11 But as she was feeding him, he grabbed her and demanded, "Come to bed with me, my darling sister." 12 "No, my brother!" she cried. "Don't be foolish! Don't do this to me! Such wicked things aren't done in Israel. 13 Where could I go in my shame? And you would be called one of the greatest fools in Israel. Please, just speak to the king about it, and he will let you marry me." 14 But Amnon wouldn't listen to her, and since he was stronger than she was, he raped her. 15 Then suddenly Amnon's love turned to hate, and he hated her even more than he had loved her. "Get out of here!" he snarled at her. 16 "No, no!" Tamar cried. "Sending me away now is worse than what you've already done to me." But Amnon wouldn't listen to her. 17 He shouted for his servant and demanded, "Throw this woman out, and lock the door behind her!" (NLT)

"I" Can Relate

These two examples should help us evaluate our voluntary relationships. We can seek the Lord about who we have wrongfully opened ourselves up to or obligated ourselves to. God is faithful to help us remove relationships from our lives that we have invited in when we were not "**AT**" the right place or time to enter into them. There are also times when God will remove them without us having a part in it at all. God is also faithful to give us wisdom when we ask so that we will understand our true obligation to Him and not others. In being obligated to our obedience to God, we will serve others according to His will, and not be obligated to them wrongfully. God can repair or remove our voluntary relationships as we allow Him to show us where we are "**AT**".

"I" Can Relate

When I look over my life, I can recall so many times when I did not stop to consider where "**I**" was "**AT**". This caused me to start in the wrong direction so many times thinking that I was ok. The Lord has even allowed me to clearly see when I was on a spiritual low and rushed to gratify my flesh instead of feeding my spirit, when the flesh never satisfies me. I have been disappointed in people and religion, and took it out on God. I am sure this is a cycle most of us can relate to.

> God will remove relationships without us having a part in it at all.

We are driven away from the Lord by things we have wrongly associated with Him, only to realize it was Him we needed in the first place to bring clarity to the situation. God is so faithful to lovingly guide us to truth, and show us how relationship with Him is the only thing that will truly satisfy long-term.

I can also relate to being emotionally depleted. Not realizing that I was empty and looking for anything or anyone to show

32

me the emotional connection I craved. Whew, "**I**" wish I could not relate. God's love has always come to fill me up again when I realized that looking everywhere else was pointless. He is enough. The Lord is all we need when we rest in His word, recognizing His love and endless thoughts and plans for our lives. I am glad I can relate to that…the love of my heavenly Father.

I need your help,
to see my way through.

I need your help,
to know what to do.

I need your guidance,
to navigate through the pain.

I need your guidance,
to see clearly through my emotional strain.

I need your wisdom,
to give me spiritual insight.

I need your wisdom,
to know when I am not right.

I need you...God

WLS

3

RELATI"*ON*"SHIP

Ask Yourself 'What is this response based "ON"?

EACH OF US ARE UNIQUELY CREATED by God. The word of God declares that we are fearfully and wonderfully made. Even the world has shown in science that we each have a one-of-a-kind fingerprint and retinal-print (eye signature). We are special to God and He deals with us based on how He created us and who He created us to be when we are His in Christ Jesus.

On top of our uniqueness in our Creator God, we also have thoughts, ideas, & reactions based on what we have experienced in this life. Our past, previous or current relationships, other people, past hurts or loss, perspective, and the junk we take in everyday through media all play a role in our responses in each situation. There are unconscious and conscious queues that cause us to react to every situation we encounter. As in everything else that we have to sift through in this life, we have to rely on the Lord to help us make sure that each action or reaction is based "ON" the present. God is the God of today. He is with us every moment. He will never leave us or forsake us. So let's look at how we can effectively navigate our responses in lieu of what we have or are going through in our life of relationships.

> Unconscious and conscious queues cause us to react to every situation we encounter.

A Previous Relationship/Somebody Else

We cannot move through this life without having relationships with other people. As we discussed last chapter, these relationships can be voluntary or involuntary. These relationships can also have been good or bad, and some inconsequential. Each relationship has the potential to affect us in some capacity.

These previous relationships can trigger responses to our current situations based **"ON"** how somebody else treated us. This possibility of reacting to a person who we are currently in relationship with based on the previous person is an opportunity to make sure we are using our *right* relationship with the Lord to guide our response. It is always right to check our words before we speak them. It is always right to sift our intentions through the filter of the Holy Spirit.

> Sift your intentions through the filter of the Holy Spirit.

We cannot take our words back. We cannot leave up to chance having an unconscious reaction to our current situation based on somebody else. God is ready, willing and able to help us realize who we are dealing with currently, and provide us with the power to act in the now so that we can have a fruitful relationship in our present.

A Past Hurt/Loss

When we have been hurt in the past, our hearts and minds can consciously or unconsciously put up barriers to present relationships. Loss of a loved one who we were in relationship with can have the same affect. These are both issues of the heart. Choosing not to be in relationship when we are not **"AT"** a good place is correct. When our heart is hurt and it has experienced loss, it needs to be healed by the Mender of Broken Hearts. That mender is God. If we do not allow time for this heart surgery by the great Physician, we will more than likely be dysfunctional within a relationship based "**ON**" that hurt or loss. God loves us and is waiting for us to come to him with our hurt and loss. In our uniqueness we each have a process that has to take place so that we will surrender this pain to God and start forgiving. Hurt and loss can call for us to not only forgive others, but ourselves and sometimes we also harbor un-forgiveness against God because the pain happened. He understands all of this and will patiently love us through our process. God wants to ease our pain and love us back to a whole place so we can be right in our relationships.

Surrender the pain to God and start forgiving.

It is common knowledge that hurt people, hurt people. That is not the way God desires our relationships to be as His children. He wants healed and whole people who can love and not hurt. God commands us to love ourselves and to love one another. He will help us to heal and love our "**I**" again so we can love one another.

Perspective

Perspective can be purely based on our "**I**". In relationships, one of the biggest lessons to learn is that each person has their own unique perspective on the situations that occur within the relationship. You can talk to a person whom you were in relationship with years before and each of you might recant a story drastically different, when you were both there and in the middle of it. An individual's perspective is usually tainted by previous experiences and their current mental, emotional, or physical state. God tells us in His word that He will guide us with His own eye. If we seek Him in this way we will find that our perspective can become clear to see through those previous experiences and our current mental, emotional and physical state. If we utilize the practice of sifting our response through God's perspective, then we can be free to base our response "**ON**" the truth of today. The

Lord will give us wisdom and help us to see clearly and build our ability to see other's points of view, helping us to become mediators and regulators of misconception in relationship.

Junk (cares of this world)

Mark 4[18] .... they are the ones who hear the word, [19] and the cares of this world, the deceitfulness of riches, and the desires for other things entering in choke the word, and it becomes unfruitful. (NKJV)

Our relationships can be wonderful and everything can be going well. Living in this world there is always a chance that the cares of this world can weigh on you and cause you to act out of the character of Christ. We as children of God are given the power by God to exhibit the fruit of the Spirit. God's word grows us and matures this fruit in our lives if we allow it to. It is a choice. Day by day we can be bombarded by issues, problems, tests, trials and unsettling interactions with people places and things. God knows this. God sees this. He also has given us everything we need for life and godliness (2 Peter 1:3).

> Don't allow Satan to infiltrate your relationships, use the power of God to overcome him.

So when junk comes to clutter and stink up your relationships, do not allow it to choke the word of God that is working within you to help you maintain a fruitful relationship. Let the junk stay right where it belongs, in the trash to be hauled away. We must not allow Satan to infiltrate our life and our relationships because we have the power of God to overcome him. We can base our relationship response **"ON"** the fruit of the Spirit, and not the junk of this world.

Stability
Is my response valid for this present Relationship?

The ability to navigate our responses to the current situation shows our maturity and stability in Christ Jesus. When we *consistently practice* evaluating the different aspects of our "**I**" in R E L A T I O N S H I P, then we can become more and more stable giving the proper response to the current situation. So, if we are close to the Lord in our *right* position through Christ, and we are choosing the prompting of the Holy Spirit over our flesh, we can respond in a way that will nurture our relationships in love. We can be clear in the light of the Lord that we are basing our response "**ON**" what is valid for the current relationship.

"I" Can Relate

"The main characteristic which is the proof of the indwelling Spirit is an amazing tenderness in personal dealing, and a blazing truthfulness with regard to God's Word." – Oswald Chambers in Disciples Indeed

Can you relate to realizing that you were "tripping", AFTER you had already said hurtful words to someone you love? I can relate. I could not take those words back. I used to be known for being blunt and saying whatever "**I**" thought needed to be said. Thank God for the Holy Spirit and the many lessons I have had to learn showing me that it is not about what "**I**" think needs to be said, but what God knows I should say, or not say. It is a beautiful thing to see how God has worked on a person's heart and you know that if you would have said what you wanted, the results would have been drastically different. God is gentle and kind. "**I**" in my flesh am not. I need Him to help me deal with others in the fruit of the Spirit, by His Spirit as I walk with Him obediently.

"I" Can Relate

Do you see me?
Am I who you are talking to?
..or does she still haunt you
even though it has been a year or two?

Do you hear me?
Or are they words from the past,
clouding your responses
....causing this relationship not to last.

Can I see you
through my past hurt and pain?
Or am I blinded
afraid it will happen again?

Do I hear your words of love,
Or are they lost to the lies of the past
...always afraid things won't last.

WLS

4

"RE"LATIONSHIP

Ask Yourself 'Am I repeating a pattern'?

THE PREFIX **RE** CAN MEAN AGAIN. By our very nature we can find comfort in routine. We can tend to gravitate toward what is familiar. Familiarity can feel right but be wrong for us in relationships.

The "**RE**" in relationship asks us to look at ourselves in the light of God's love and guidance to discover if we are repeating a wrong pattern of behavior. God can help us see if we are doing the same things over and over again, expecting things to get better in our relationships, when these actions are not allowing them to. There are four areas that we will discuss that we might need to bring before God to see if they are a part of our pattern or routine in our relationships. We might be using familiar habits such as *manipulation, desperation, false expectation, or isolation* unconsciously. These mindsets can be **strongholds** that repeatedly sabotage our relationships. God's word has something to say about all of these. Let's utilize our relationship with Him to search our hearts in these areas.

> Familiarity can feel right but be wrong in relationships.

Manipulation
This is one of the most prevalent behaviors in humans that can seem very innocent and cause you to be the last one to detect it in your own behavior. Manipulation is very subtle.

"I" Can Relate

Manipulation is rooted in selfishness, which has nothing to do with God. Let us look at a biblical example of manipulation from one of our patriarchs in the faith lineage.

Genesis 27 [1] One day when Isaac was old and turning blind, he called for Esau, his older son, and said, "My son." "Yes, Father?" Esau replied.[2] "I am an old man now," Isaac said, "and I don't know when I may die. [3] Take your bow and a quiver full of arrows, and go out into the open country to hunt some wild game for me. [4] Prepare my favorite dish, and bring it here for me to eat. Then I will pronounce the blessing that belongs to you, my firstborn son, before I die."[5] But Rebekah overheard what Isaac had said to his son Esau. So when Esau left to hunt for the wild game, [6] she said to her son Jacob, "Listen. I overheard your father say to Esau, [7] 'Bring me some wild game and prepare me a delicious meal. Then I will bless you in the Lord's presence before I die.'[8] Now, my son, listen to me. Do exactly as I tell you. [9] Go out to the flocks, and bring me two fine young goats. I'll use them to prepare your father's favorite dish. [10] Then take the food to your father so he can eat it and bless you before he dies."[11] "But look," Jacob replied to Rebekah, "my brother, Esau, is a hairy man, and my skin is smooth. [12] What if my father touches me? He'll see that I'm trying to trick him, and then he'll curse me instead of blessing me."[13] But his mother replied, "Then let the curse fall on me, my son! Just do what I tell you. Go out and get the goats for me!"[14] So Jacob went out and got the young goats for his mother. Rebekah took them and prepared a delicious meal, just the way Isaac liked it. [15] Then she took Esau's favorite clothes, which were there in the house, and gave them to her younger son, Jacob. [16] She covered his arms and the smooth part of his neck with the skin of the young goats. [17] Then she gave Jacob the delicious meal, including freshly baked bread.[18] So Jacob took the food to his father. "My father?" he said."Yes, my son," Isaac answered. "Who are you—Esau or Jacob?"[19] Jacob replied, "It's Esau, your firstborn son. I've done as you told me. Here is the wild game. Now sit up and eat it so you can give me your blessing."[20] Isaac asked, "How did you find it so quickly, my son?" "The Lord your God put it in my path!" Jacob replied.[21] Then Isaac said to Jacob, "Come closer so I can touch you and make sure that you really are Esau." [22] So Jacob went closer to his father, and

Isaac touched him. "The voice is Jacob's, but the hands are Esau's," Isaac said.²³ But he did not recognize Jacob, because Jacob's hands felt hairy just like Esau's. So Isaac prepared to bless Jacob. ²⁴ "But are you really my son Esau?" he asked."Yes, I am," Jacob replied.²⁵ Then Isaac said, "Now, my son, bring me the wild game. Let me eat it, and then I will give you my blessing." So Jacob took the food to his father, and Isaac ate it. He also drank the wine that Jacob served him. ²⁶ Then Isaac said to Jacob, "Please come a little closer and kiss me, my son."²⁷ So Jacob went over and kissed him. And when Isaac caught the smell of his clothes, he was finally convinced, and he blessed his son. He said, "Ah! The smell of my son is like the smell of the outdoors, which the Lord has blessed! ²⁸ "From the dew of heaven and the richness of the earth, may God always give you abundant harvests of grain and bountiful new wine. ²⁹ May many nations become your servants, and may they bow down to you. May you be the master over your brothers, and may your mother's sons bow down to you. All who

Manipulation is rooted in selfishness, & has nothing to do with God.

curse you will be cursed, and all who bless you will be blessed."
³⁰ As soon as Isaac had finished blessing Jacob, and almost before Jacob had left his father, Esau returned from his hunt. ³¹ Esau prepared a delicious meal and brought it to his father. Then he said, "Sit up, my father, and eat my wild game so you can give me your blessing."³² But Isaac asked him, "Who are you?" Esau replied, "It's your son, your firstborn son, Esau."³³ Isaac began to tremble uncontrollably and said, "Then who just served me wild game? I have already eaten it, and I blessed him just before you came. And yes, that blessing must stand!"³⁴ When Esau heard his father's words, he let out a loud and bitter cry. "Oh my father, what about me? Bless me, too!" he begged.³⁵ But Isaac said, "Your brother was here, and he tricked me. He has taken away your blessing."³⁶ Esau exclaimed, "No wonder his name is Jacob, for now he has cheated me twice. First he took my rights as the firstborn, and now he has stolen my blessing. Oh, haven't you saved even one blessing for me?"(NLT)

Since Jacob (who God later named Israel) is one of our examples of faith and walking with God, we can be sure to feel no condemnation when we have manipulated in the past. God's love granted us forgiveness on the cross through His blood, and no past or present sin can separate us from Him. Nor can it stop us from regaining closeness in our relationship with Him if we repent. Once we ask the Lord to show us if this is a pattern that is harming not only our

> God help us see if we are doing the same things over & over again, expecting it to get better.

relationship with Him, but also with others, He will be faithful to lovingly set the right process in motion to reveal and heal us of this dysfunction in relationship. We can have a wrong understanding of how God wants us to communicate and submit to Him, and unconsciously utilize *manipulative prayers* and *conditional obedience* with Him. The Lord is holy and is not subject to this human behavior, but He does have compassion and grace for it so that He will show us that it will not bear fruit, and we can correct it in our actions towards Him. This process will in turn shine light on the behavior in our other relationships, helping us to correct the unproductive pattern there also.

Desperation

Jeremiah 2[23] "You say, 'That's not true! I haven't worshiped the images of Baal!' But how can you say that? Go and look in any valley in the land! Face the awful sins you have done. You are like a restless female camel desperately searching for a mate. [24] You are like a wild donkey, sniffing the wind at mating time. Who can restrain her lust? Those who desire her don't need to search, for she goes running to them! [25] When will you stop running? When will you stop panting after other gods? But you say, 'Save your breath. I'm in love with these foreign gods, and I can't stop loving them now!' (NLT)

What has stolen your heart from God, so much that you believe it is the only answer? That is where desperation stems from, not trusting God with your life and love. God is trustworthy and His love will alleviate your desperation for all the idols, or other things you have elevated to that important place in your life. Remember an idol can be anything you think you cannot live without. An idol can be anything that you think is the only answer to your frustration, desperation, or expectation. As a child of God you are never desperate, even if you feel that way, re-focusing on your true source, God, can bring peace with that truth.

God tells us that He will not withhold any good things from those who walk uprightly. Remember we are "right" through the blood of Jesus, and when we walk, or obey the Holy Spirit and not our flesh, we are walking upright. The feeling of desperation is a trick of the enemy, Satan. When there is a desire in us that has not been fulfilled, wrong thinking, distractions, wrong advice, and worldly falsehoods can lead us to believe that we are out of options. With God and by the leading of the Holy Spirit, we can center ourselves on the love of God and His sovereignty, allowing us to see the truth. Is this easy? No. That is why we have the Lord to empower us through the promises of His word and the encouragement of other believers to persevere. David said in psalms 27:13, that he would have fainted if he did not believe that he would see the goodness of the Lord in the land of the living. This sentiment has to resound in our hearts, as it is one of the jobs of the Holy Spirit to bring the remembrance of God's word to our minds. If we believe that God will not withhold things that are good for us from us, and that we will see His good while we are here on earth, then we can continue calling the devil a liar and casting desperation far from our heart and mind.

> An idol can be anything you think you cannot live without.

The Lord is near us and has exactly what we need in every area of our lives. Trust in God kills desperation. Leaning not on our own understanding, knowing it can be based on the lies of this world, smothers desperation. When we are close to the Lord we know and can fight any attack that brings desperation to our hearts. Desperation is a lie, and we can speak to it with the love and comfort of God knowing He that is within us (Holy Spirit) is greater than all the lies of this world.

Expectation
Proverbs 10:[28] The hopes of the godly result in happiness, but the expectations of the wicked come to nothing. (NLT)

We serve a God that wants us to daily "expect" Him to be our Father, our Guide, our Protector, our Love, our Comfort, our Healer and our Counselor. God is our All in All, and is whatever we need. When we put our expectations in anyone else or anything else, we will be disappointed either immediately or eventually. Doing this sets us up for frustration, disappointment and pain. We all have or have had *false or wrong expectations*. These false expectations in relationship can stem from many places. We can believe or expect men or women will be or do things based on past experiences, what our family showed and taught us, or by what we have seen either on TV or in our own lives. These expectations can be repeated or reinforced by how others have treated us in the past. We can also repeat them if we don't understand that they are harmful and are not put into perspective in the light of the truth of the word of God. When we ask the Lord to show us if we are expecting things from others that only He can fulfill, then He can and will shine a light on them if

> Expectation in anyone else sets us up for frustration, disappointment and pain.

we allow Him to do so. Only then can we evaluate and mend relationships that have been broken by us expecting the other person to perform, provide for or do things that only God can do. Yes He uses people here on earth to bless His children, but we are not to assume to know by whom or through what He will send the blessing or provision. We are to expect God to bless and provide for us, but we are to allow Him to be God and do it the way He pleases. In His love we are free to trust Him, and then release others we are in relationship with from wrong expectations, allowing us to love them for who they are and without conditions.

We can also have a wrong expectation of who God is and what He will or will not do. God has given us the bible as the best source of knowing Him, His character, His ways, and what to expect from Him. It is our job to seek His wisdom there, to seek Him in prayer, in meditation and in expecting His love and promises to manifest in our lives. God tells us that when we seek Him we will find Him. When we know this and do it, we will not be subject

> Expect God to bless and provide for you, but allow Him to do it the way He pleases.

to wrong teaching that causes us to expect wrongly and become disappointed and frustrated. God has the power to reveal His ways and the character of His love in many different ways and through many different means. He will show us if we expect Him to and open ourselves up to Him outside of the confines of religion and tradition. God is always doing a new thing, and we must be willing to have our understanding constantly grow, building on the foundation of Jesus. His will is always in love, even if we cannot understand it immediately. We are told that His ways are not our ways and His thoughts are not our thoughts. Some things will be beyond our comprehension until we see Him face to face, but we still must trust and expect His love to manifest in our lives and in our relationships.

As we ask the Lord to reveal our false or wrong expectations in every area, we will see that we will receive understanding in its time. God's love knows exactly what process it will take to reveal these wrong expectations to us as we can bear it. With each enlightenment we will have the opportunity to allow God to change our mindset and deliver us from a pattern of constantly expecting others to do what only He can.

Isolation

Leviticus 13[46] As long as the serious disease lasts, they will be ceremonially unclean. They must live in isolation in their place outside the camp. (NLT)

Let's look at that word disease. *Dis-ease*. When we have been hurt, betrayed, infected by the world, and overcome with all of the ills of this world, we are *dis-eased*. We need the Lord to clean us up so we will move from the wrong place of isolation we have been driven to, or allowed ourselves to stay. Only Christ can clean us up, mend our hearts, help us forgive, and teach us to receive His love and love others again.

> We have to choose to NOT be ok with things the way they were before God.

others again. Jesus came that we do not have to be "unclean" or soiled by sin and separated from God. His blood cleanses us when we accept Him, and from that moment of acceptance we can start allowing Him to work in us cleaning us up from our dealings in this world.

As children of God we are spiritually clean in Jesus, being forgiven of sin, period. Unfortunately we can become entangled again in what the word of God calls the *old man's* behavior, forgetting that we have been cleansed and set on a new path to live in a new way. This behavior that can lead us into sin or sinful thoughts and actions is not insurmountable in comparison to the power of Christ. We just have to choose to not wallow in what is familiar, comfortable, or easy. We have to choose to not be *ok* with things as they were in our lives before God. This *passivity or double mindedness* can lead us to either physically isolating ourselves or spiritual isolation by not taking a stand in God's word calling upon the power He has given us.

"I" Can Relate

In this section I encourage you to ask the Lord to show you these repeating patterns that you might have in relationships. I am still asking God myself to show me and convict me if I enter into this familiar defeating behavior. This work of the Holy Spirit is continuous, but it does get easier as the Lord removes our tendencies in the areas of manipulation, acts of desperation, and hiding away in isolation when we have wrong expectations. "**I**" can relate to the comfort of familiar behaviors, but I will not keep resorting to them when I know I have the power to overcome them. I want the newness of stable and consistent behavior in my relationships. I want to know that love is the driving factor, not manipulation. I want to trust God to heal my heart with the understanding that I can never be desperate when I am in His hands. I know my spirit can relate to always expecting great things from a God who is always with me guiding me to greater relationship.

"I" Can Relate

Am I doing it again?
I'm not sure....
I need you Oh Lord,
To keep my heart pure.

Am I doing it again?
I don't want to hurt anybody.
It is happening again...

Can you show me please,
the pattern I must break.

Can you help me Oh Lord,
for my relationships sake.

I can't do it again,
I need your relief.

I won't do it again,
Your love will help me not repeat
the same mistakes
...that make my heart ache.

Never again,
My emotions won't win.
Your love will guide me,
with your Holy Spirit inside me.

WLS

5

RELATION"SHIP"

Ask Yourself 'Where is this taking me & the person "I" am in relationship with'?

HAVE YOU CONSIDERED THAT YOU might be allowing yourself to be taken down paths that you don't really want to go just to be in a relationship? Have you also considered that you might be harming your brother or sister by involving them in a relationship when you know you are not "**AT**" a place where you should be in relationship?

Galatians 5[13] For you have been called to live in freedom, my brothers and sisters. But don't use your freedom to satisfy your sinful nature. Instead, use your freedom to serve one another in love. [14] For the whole law can be summed up in this one command: "Love your neighbor as yourself." (NLT)

How are you managing your reactions? What are you basing them "**ON**"? Have you let your desire to be in a relationship be led by wrong motives, that have un-intentionally taken you places you have been convicted not to go?

The "**SHIP**" in relationship can take you down traitorous waters that can have your life turning up-side down with every high wave, flowing in the wrong direction with every misguided emotion, and heading toward a shipwreck that your heart can't stand again. The relationships God wants you to be in should bring you and the other person closer to Him. The relationships that He does not want you to be in can take you toward sin, moving you further and further from His will and blessings for your life. My "**I**" has been in both of these relational situations. It can be easy to enter into and stay in the wrong relationship if you are not doing the evaluating and sifting we have been discussing in previous chapters of your "**I**" in each relationship. Remember it can be a struggle since the flesh is contrary to the spirit, but it does not have to be when we are being intentional to consult the Holy Spirit each step of the way. It takes a sincere heart toward God and loving Him more than you love yourself to allow Him to guide your relation"ships". It also takes trust. It is very easy for us as humans to think we know what is best for us, or even feel like we

Do you feel you can manipulate the person toward God & not sin?

can manipulate the person or situation toward God instead of sin. The problem with these thoughts is that they cause you to lean toward your own understanding…this is dangerous. We are to trust in the Lord with all our hearts, and believe that if a relationship is not right for us, we should not get on board under false pretenses or expectations. If we are in "right" relationship with the Lord, staying close to Him, we can make sure we choose the right relationship that takes us toward God's will being done in our *life* and in our relationship as it is in heaven.

The relation"ships" we are discussing here are not only male/female dating relationships in this section. Misguided relationships can come in all forms. We can also entertain friendships with other males or females that can become "ship"wrecks as well. I mention this here as a word of caution, because we can also form attachments to friendships for the wrong reasons which can lead or persuade us away from God. The rest of this chapter will primarily focus on male/female relationships, but there is also always opportunity for the Holy Spirit to speak to you on friendships as well.

There are many books that attempt to answer questions concerning whether "we should date or court?" "Is dating wrong for a Christian?" "Should I allow my teenager to date?" So this is not that book. The late Dr. Myles Munroe has a great book on dating that I recommend if that is a topic you want to explore. Here we **"SHIPS" can take** are looking at relationships, so **us closer to God or** there is an assumption that you have been in one or are **toward sin.** currently in one, whether you call it dating or courting. In this book we are concerned with how you are treating or handling your "I" within the relationship. Remember these "SHIPS" can potentially take us closer to God or toward sin. There are two factors we can look at that will be barometers for us as we decipher which way we are going. These two factors are time and treatment.

The Holy Spirit's Work
As in all aspect of our *life* in relationship we have to realize the importance of the work of God in us during the relationship. We can become focused on what the other person should be doing or fixing, but God wants us listening to the promptings of the Holy Spirit in us. This is how we can learn and know how to navigate the **"SHIP"** or abandon the **"SHIP"**.

Whether we are looking at time or treatment, the Lord has to give us wisdom and guide us through our individual situation and process in truth. Grace and truth manifest through our relationship with Jesus Christ, and it is in this relationship that the Holy Spirit will work to bring those two, grace and truth, to the forefront of each relationship.

Time

Time can be looked at in a couple of different ways. In relationships we can look at how long we have known a person, but typically this is not as big a factor as how much personal time we spend on a daily basis with the person. Larger amounts of personal intimate, one-on-one time are more influential in relationship then the length of years with someone. When we are spending time with God, one-on-one quiet time praying and meditating on His word, our relationship with Him is stronger.

We can learn how to navigate the "SHIP" or abandon the "SHIP".

When we spend this time with God we typically hear, understand and obey what the Holy Spirit is trying to say to us in situations better day to day. This is because we have been spending time nurturing our relationship with the Lord, because we value it. In this life, time is a commodity, so when you decide to spend one-on-one personal time with someone you are telling them they are important.

You can also be with a person alone, but not really be spending time with them. This time can be looked at in its quantity, but has no quality. In relationships like this, we can feel like we might as well be alone. The amount of hours alone with a person when you are not communicating or they are not relating to you should not be counted as time valued at all. My **"I"** has been in relationship and felt like I was alone. The other person cannot value you or your time by always putting you last in priority with other things and people in his or her life. This *can* also look like him or her not paying attention to you when you are together by texting, being on the computer or phone, or watching TV.

Another example worth looking at as far as time is concerned is when the person is emotionally or physically trying to isolate you by taking up your time so that you cannot see or relate to anyone else. This can be emotional manipulation of your time so you will feel guilty if you spend it with anyone else, or physical manipulation when they don't allow you to see or relate to anyone else either by threat of violence or moving you away from everyone you know so it is hard to get to see them. If either of these is happing to you there can be a larger more urgent issue at hand, and I hope that this will encourage you to abandon **"SHIP'** and find a local hotline or shelter that can help you navigate to a safe place in relationship where you are not being harmed physically or emotionally.

You can have quantity, but no quality.

Time itself can be deceptive emotionally if we put more value on the quantity of it, and not the quality of it. For most people, time equates to caring, so there is the possibility that an emotional attachment can begin to form with time spent. Remember time spent can be just quantity and be filled with negativity. Emotions themselves are from God, therefore they are good. But they can be misguided and misleading if not sifted through the Holy Spirit. In relationship, emotional attachments can be formed when they should not be and become a *stronghold* when it is time to abandon a relationship.

Whether your time is valued and well spent, or if it is not valued and manipulated, there should never be an occasion when time spent with the person you are in relationship with totally wipes out your time that could be spent with God. There has to be some type of balance. God acknowledges that in marriage the woman can be caught up with the cares of her husband, but that is only in the institution of marriage, not before. There can be a tendency in this world to do things out of order, and God is a God of order who blesses His children when we obey Him and trust Him by patiently waiting for each step in the process of relationship. If we are not married we have to intentionally make sure that we are establishing a practice of spending one-on-one time with the Lord in proportion to time with the person we are in relationship with. This is very important for many reasons when we factor in the impact of time on relationship.

We are influenced most by the people we spend the most time with. This is especially true when it is quality one-on-one time, and we love, value or care for that person. Unfortunately, this can be true even if we are spending time with a person in a negative or manipulative relationship. So if we are spending large quantities of time with a person in relationship we could be influenced more by that person and their way of thinking than God and His way of thinking. We must balance our time between the two. It

> Don't be fooled into thinking that your "I" is exempt from getting "ship"wrecked due to mismanagement of time.

is a matter of priority and choice. Being susceptible to the influence of the persons we spend a lot of time with is human nature, and no one is exempt. It does not matter what you gifting is, skill or ability as a child of God, ALL will be more susceptible to being led toward sin if there is not an intentional effort to spend more time with God in order to keep our minds renewed. Our spiritual life has to be nurtured by time with God. You could be preaching every Sunday or teaching bible study every Wednesday, and even doing ministry to feed the hungry once a week and still have your spiritual life eroded by the person you are spending most of your time with in relationship. We must not be fooled as children of God that our "I" is exempt from getting "ship"wrecked due to mismanagement of time.

Treatment

Treatment is the second factor that has to be evaluated in conjunction with time. How are you allowing your "I" to be treated in your relationships? What are your expectations of how you are supposed to be treated? This is a fundamental understanding that has to be learned and enforced through us being in a close personal relationship with God. This is what we discussed in chapter one, which dealt with getting to know our *self* in light of who God says we are and what He has planned for us as His child. If we don't have expectations relating to God's love and blessings in our *life*, we will allow our *self* to be treated any kind of way. If we don't know our value and worth to God, then we might not value our own *self* and allow our *self* to be treated any kind of way. How much we know and understand the God-factor in our *life* determines how much mistreatment we will allow. This can only be combated with one-on-one time with God growing in love, trust and understanding.

> Our spiritual life has to be nurtured by time with God.

Sometimes it can be hard to recognize when we are being mistreated. Maybe the way we are being treated is the way we have seen our mother treat our father, or our father treat our mother; so it *appears* to be ok. We can also base whether we are being treated well by relationship examples we have seen growing up, whether that was on TV, in movies or the way our friends or people we looked up to were treated. So what do you do if all of those examples exhibited relationships that were dysfunctional, and one or both of the persons were being mistreated? We look to our heavenly Father to show us the truth. God is able to show us how we should be treated as we interact with Him and accept His love.

"I" Can Relate

Did you know that if you have been treated poorly all your life it is hard to accept being treated well? When we are poorly treated, it can cause us to devalue our *self*, and we might not even realize that this treatment is wrong. We can become conditioned to being mistreated. There are instances when we do not know any different. In these situations we can unconsciously devalue ourselves and not expect anything better, or desire anything more. The only thing that can change this is an encounter with the love of the living God. Exposure to and experience with the love of God through Jesus Christ will awaken your heart to *something more*. The love of God is powerful. The sacrifice and teaching of Jesus can do an indescribable work in your heart that will start you down a path that can change everything you know and every relationship you have. Growing in a personal relationship with God will not only give you an understanding of how He treats you, but the Lord will also place people in your life who will treat you in the godly way He empowers through the fruit of the spirit. God has people and places for your life. If you allow the Holy Spirit to guide your "I", the Lord will lead you to people and places in relationship that will amaze you.

How do you expect to be treated?

There are those of us who believe we have been treated well. God never ceases to amaze me in this relationship journey, because just when you think you have the best friends or have had the best relationships with the opposite gender, God will introduce a feeling or desire in you that says with God there is something more. With God all things are possible, and He wants each of us to experience the love He has for us through His other children in relationship. We should never stop expecting more out of God when it comes to the way we as His children should be treated in God ordained relationships.

Does this mean we are not going to be mistreated? No. Jesus warns us that if we follow Him in this world we will have troubles, and that some people will hate us for loving Him and following Him; but that does not mean that God does not have relationships that will bless and amaze us as we move through this life.

As we look at time spent in our relationships, we also have to factor in how we are treated or how we treat others in those times. The two cannot be separated as we present them to God and sift our understanding of them with the Holy Spirit. In the time spent were we mostly operating in our flesh, sinning against God? In the time spent did we recognize the love of God in them because we know it from our time spent with the Lord? In the time spent

God has people and places for our *life*.

in relationship, were we glorifying God in the way we were getting to know each other? In the relationship are we each learning what it means to be a child of God in the Kingdom of God and sharing it with each other? Does this relationship help me grow as we spend time together, or does it always lead me to feeling defeated and needing to repent? Does this relationship challenge my character and drive me to the Holy Spirit to check my reactions and interactions. Am I being gentle and kind? Am I encouraging sin with the person I am in relationship? Am I exhibiting forgiveness and humility in this relationship? Use these questions and the two barometers of time and treatment to evaluate before God if you need to abandon the relationship or navigate it in another direction.

Grace
We have to remember grace in every relationship. God gives us grace. If we recognize His grace in our lives, then we are more likely to allow the Holy Spirit to give us the power to give grace to others. So what is grace? Grace, in the word of

God, is what God has granted us by the sacrifice of His Son Jesus Christ. Because of this sacrifice we are forgiven when there is no reason for us to be. Grace can encompass all the areas in our lives where God gives us undeserved favor or help, instead of leaving us

> Remember grace in every relationship.

alone to fight for ourselves in this world. Grace is the power to overcome sin, grace is the power to keep going, grace is love for the unlovable, and grace is all sufficient for everything we face in the world and in our relationships.

In relationship we can be on either side of the situation, the catalyst toward sin or the catalyst toward God. There is grace for both. In relationship there always has to be room for forgiveness and mercy. Knowing that God grants us his forgiveness and mercy on a daily basis, we can count on the Holy Spirit to give us the power to choose to show forgiveness and mercy to those whom we are in relationship with.

"I" Can Relate

"The measure of the worth of our public activity for God is the private profound communion we have with Him.... We have to pitch our tents where we shall always have quiet times with God, however noisy our times with the world may be." – Oswald Chambers in My Utmost for His Highest, January 6

"I" can truly relate to needing the Lord for balance. I love to be in love and spending time in relationship is one of my favorite things. I am sure that is one of the reasons why the Lord has taken me through some very extended times alone, to teach me balance and reliance on Him. God has a specific process for each of us to help us realize our motivations and dysfunctions in relation"ships". I have gotten so much clarity in my one-on-one set aside time with the Lord. Do I have to remind myself to make it happen? Yes. God wants to guide our relationships, but we have the responsibility to seek Him for that guidance. When I seek Him first, I am able to see when I am following a misguided emotion. When I seek Him first, I am able to discern if my actions or the actions of the person I am in relationship with is taking us in the wrong direction. I don't have to allow myself to get tossed around when God can lead me beside still waters. It is a choice. I wish I couldn't relate to getting swept away by what looked good and felt good. But I can.

We can be on either side of the situation, the catalyst toward sin or the catalyst toward God.

But because of God and His guidance I can say *Not Anymore*!

Should I trust you?

Is this relationship safe?

Am I ready to share my heart?
....or will I cause yours to break?

Do we need to go there?
...or is this the wrong path.

I will say a little prayer,
for your Holy Spirit to guide me.

Maybe I am not ready,
I know You can show me the way
....my heart needs time.

Thank you Lord,
Your love and guidance eases my mind.

WLS

AFTERWARD

S O YOU MIGHT BE ASKING WHAT DO I DO NOW? Move forward. Allow the Holy Spirit to convict you as you read different parts of this book over again. Another great thing to do is to use a journal and write out your past friendships and male/female relationships. Then you can look at them honestly and ask the Lord to show you any repeating patterns or incorrect responses that may have sabotaged those relationships. The Lord can also show you which relationships you grew in and learned from. Journaling as you re-read this book can open your eyes by God's spirit to new revelation on your "I", and lead you to many blessings in current and future relationships.

The information in this book is to be reflected on and put into constant practice. The most important message is to stay close to God through your personal relationship with Jesus. This will allow you to sift through all things and make consistent and thoughtful choices in relationship. God's Holy Spirit is in you for a reason. This is the abiding that God desires. He wants to be your constant companion, lover and friend.

God bless you in your journey in, through and out of relationships. Remember there is a time for everything, so there will be times that we are not in close relationship with anyone but God. Cherish that time, knowing that He is growing you and loving you for *something more* in relationship.

Wanda
www.wandalscott.com

OTHER RESOURCES BY WANDA L. SCOTT

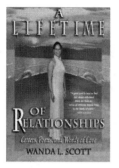

Where are you in life's relationships?

What have you been through in your lifetime?

"A good poet is hard to find and welcome when she finds us. Let us welcome Wanda Scott to the family of poets." *Nikki Giovanni*

A Lifetime of Relationships: Letters, Poems and Words of Love is an evolution and exploration into the life of Wanda L. Scott, a journey through the tumultuous emotions of life's experiences. It is a compilation of passionate poetry reflecting on life and love, pain and powerlessness, highs and lows. This book touches you where you are in life's relationships. It will help others to reflect on their life and inquire how they can express themselves to release life's emotions.

Life has a unique way of entangling us in the midst of our relationships and emotions. Are you ready to move through life releasing instead of storing up the pain? How do you express yourself in these emotional times? How do you move past the emotional pain to spiritual healing, true love, and peace? One way is to express ourselves with letters, poems and words of love.

A Lifetime of Relationships is a vehicle to demonstrate God's power of creative expression through his children, and has a **companion workshop** that stresses *God's Word on Godly Relationships.*

To learn more about Wanda's workshops, teachings, and other resources visit her on the Web at: www.wandalscott.com

Or write:

Wanda L. Scott
P.O. Box 120804
Nashville, TN 37212-0804